A STIFF DRINK AND A CLOSE SHAVE

BOB SLOAN *and* STEVEN GUARNACCIA

- - - - - - - - - - -

DESIGN *by* SUSAN HOCHBAUM

PHOTOGRAPHY *by* GENTL & HYERS

CHRONICLE BOOKS
SAN FRANCISCO

WE DEDICATE THIS BOOK TO

Seaver Leslie and Bill Kennedy–two men who knew how to shave.
— **B.S**.

My grandfather, Theodore D. Sulzer, who taught me everything
I know about being a man.
— **S.G.**

Library of Congress Cataloging-in-Publication Data available.
ISBN 0-8118-0757-6
Printed in Hong Kong

Book and cover design: Susan Hochbaum

Distributed in Canada by Raincoast Books,
8680 Cambie Street, Vancouver, B.C., V6P 6M9

10 9 8 7 6 5 4 3 2 1

Chronicle Books
275 Fifth Street
San Francisco, CA 94103

A

STIFF **AND** CLOSE

DRINK SHAVE

A
STIFF DRINK
AND A
CLOSE SHAVE

SHAVING

Since most men shave more often than they make love, the equipment they used needed to be chosen with care—to make the experience soft and warm. Smooth, close, and comfortable.

HATS

Administering to the dents in the crown, fixing the brim at the exact angle—the final morning ritual before facing the world. Because a man knew he wasn't fully dressed unless he was wearing his hat.

CULTURE

The Cultured Male dug hard-hitting prose. Read intently sports columnists such as Grantland Rice and Jimmy Cannon. Went for the B-Picture over the Feature. Spun a couple pounds of jazz platters as a preferred evening activity.

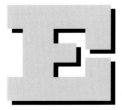

COCKTAILS

From an Asylum to a Zaza; from a Bosom Caresser to a Ward Eight, it was the job of the Man of the House to preside over the impeccably precise and slightly eccentric domain of the cocktail.

GAMBLING

Poker, ponies, and pinochle constituted much of what a man did with his leisure time. A stellar day would start with a few hands of stud, segue into the Daily Double, and reach its denouement with a torrid game of pinochle, lasting long into the night.

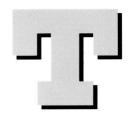

55

BLUE PLATE

Watch out, Dad's got the apron on for his yearly foray into the kitchen. Maybe he'll scramble some eggs or concoct some spectacularly mammoth sandwiches. But just wait for barbecue season—then you'll see some serious cooking.

GIRLIE

Two reasons to check the wall calendar—to count the days until payday and glom the picture of the sultry redhead supine on the haystack, the piece of gingham covering her top barely large enough to fashion a small serviette. What year is it anyway?

TOP DRAWER

A man's place to save, to stash, to conceal. No one goes in his top drawer. What's stored in there is *personal.* Proust needed cookies, but most men have in their top drawers objects that will bring back equally poignant memories.

SMOKING

A man didn't smoke casually. There was craft involved—lighter techniques, assorted butt flicks. Etiquette, too. Like lighting a woman's cigarette. And a museum's-worth of paraphernalia.

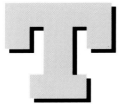

MUCH OF WHAT WE KNOW about Egyptian civilization comes from entombed artifacts, stuff buried with the Kings and Princes. Life dead for Old Pharaoh was every bit as rich as life living. In the same way, caskets packed with vintage men's paraphernalia, the stuff men used to use, would present future grave diggers with a detailed portrait of the occupations, dreams, obsessions, and hobbies of the American male, 1930-1959.

This was a time when men had a wide assortment of objects that they needed in the course of their day. Though they had no official designation, they were distinctly MEN'S STUFF—what a man really used to groom, smoke, imbibe, to hold his tie in place, to guide him through a dark basement to replace a fuse, to prevent unwanted progeny. They were not accessories, designed to add a subtle touch or graceful accent—like a pastel scarf over a black coat, for example, or a hair bow. No sir. This stuff wasn't frivolous. It was pragmatic. What a man carried in his pockets, or stored in his half of the medicine cabinet, or squirreled away in his top dresser drawer or jammed in his toolbox in the basement. And though most of these were common, everyday items, the Men's Stuff from this era infused a man's life with a sense of design and craftsmanship, of patience and sensual indulgence, of humor and whimsy.

Think of the zeitgeist of SHAVING with a brush and mug as opposed to an aerosol can. The pace is completely different. It's not about saving time, not about "quick and easy," but of relishing the experience. The soothing warmth of the lather, the feel of the natural badger brush, created the genuine experience of grooming, instead of simply getting rid of your whiskers.

The brush itself is **SUPREMELY ELEGANT**. Someone took time to design the Bakelite or stainless steel or ivory handle. Someone thought about the subtle contours and shades of the bristles that form a gently tapered crown. The mug, with its **FEMININE CURVES**, another opportunity for design, and the soap nestled neatly inside. Not a logo in sight. No slogans shouting at you, urging you on. A shave of this kind is, in a much greater sense, a unique occurrence. Something you make happen—a story, with beginning, middle, and end. Not an homage to instantaneous disposability, but theatrical in its sense of repetition, of controlled spontaneity. It wasn't just hot lather that was lost when the shaving brush was usurped.

Even the most **BLATANTLY SEXUAL** of a man's paraphernalia was distinctly tinged with innocence and humor. Take all the Girlie images, for instance. They were everywhere. Put on your tie, there she was, painted in the lining, secretly brushing against your chest all day. Write a check, the skimpy dress on the curvy dish in the top of your pen slowly slipped away. Check the temperature, there was a coy redhead, unclad except for a fur coat that barely reached her thigh, surrounding the thermometer and suggesting she was looking for someone just like you to keep her igloo warm. Painted with **AN IDEAL BEAUTY**, fabulously buxom, all legs and décolletage, smiling seductively, these girls bending over backwards (and forwards) to display their shapely forms, drawn delighted in the attention they were drawing. And even though the painting of the blond cutie in the inside of your pocket spyglass was completely naked, these Girlie images were downright tame. They were not real. They didn't attempt to be real. They were pretend and looked pretend and basically acknowledged that most men are lascivious, ogling fools.

And there was more. Lots of men, when they were kids with crew-cuts and flannel shirts and jeans with cuffs and souvenir Indian bead belts, played with **CHEMISTRY SETS** in their basements. Then, when they grew up, and had basements of their own, they set up a different kind of chemistry set. Now togged in gabardine shirts, pleated pants, and socks with no shortage of clocking, they played with their cocktail sets at their very own Bar.

THE COCKTAIL GAME had similar equipment to the chemistry set—measurers, stirrers, spoons, strainer, and shakers. There were also specific formulas that had been scientifically developed by **ESTEEMED MIXOLOGISTS**. And as with their youthful science experiments, precision was important. The recipes had to be followed to the letter. Otherwise the boss could get a Tom Collins not to his liking, putting the kibosh on more than just the dinner party. Like the chemicals, the precious and **VOLATILE BAR LIQUIDS** were held in glass containers. Powerful agents (like olives, onions, and Angostura bitters) had to be treated with great care because a tiny amount caused a powerful reaction. And just as with his most successful chemical discoveries, a man liked to share the results of his bar experiments with his friends.

There was a fantastic array of bar ware. As much equipment as the Little Woman had in her kitchen. Glasses of all sizes and shapes accommodated the different drinks, allowing for volume or ice capacity or cold retention. Martini glasses were elegantly refined. Shot and rocks glasses, purely functional. Tropical drink glasses sported painted hula dancers and were tall enough to hold a paper umbrella. In addition, bottle stops, often in glistening stainless steel, strong and modern, like a skyscraper or a streamlined train, testaments to endurance and integrity. And there were cocktail shakers with every kind of design, from **PINK ELEPHANTS** to angels. A man had to know his way around his bar, to study his drink guide, to be ready for any request. It wasn't just a casual relationship.

This was also a time when most men smoked, and there was a great deal of **SMOKING** stuff as well. Mainly cigarette cases, ashtrays, and lighters. The design and spirit of cigarette lighters have noticeably deteriorated in the last few decades. Most people today buy disposable lighters. Purely functional, hideously colored, these are basically plastic cylinders filled with butane that light your cigarette and nothing more. That's all.

But in the '40s for about three bucks, you could buy yourself a handsomely crafted pocket lighter that you'd carry for a decade, at least. It probably had some kind of design or picture on the outside—something **STRONG AND MANLY** A solitary fisherman standing in a stream, his fly rod caught mid-cast. A thoroughbred charging to the finish line. A batter striding into a fastball. **YOUR LIGHTER** reminded you of things you liked to do. Maybe it was a gift from a supplier. A token of esteem from your tire salesman. In that case their name would be printed on it somewhere and you could thank them every time you lit up.

POCKET LIGHTERS had a distinctive click when opened—a subtle, yet resonant "**PING**." With practice, you could flick the top and hit the wheel in one motion with the inside of your index finger, which became appropriately callused. Another technique was to snap the top open, then scrape the wheel on your jeans along the back of your thigh, sparking the flint and igniting the wick. You could then produce with a flourish the **FLAMING LIGHTER**. A simple pocket lighter gave a man endless potential for stylistic statements. It said something about you. You see a woman at the table across from you in the restaurant, or next to you at the bar, fumbling in her purse for a match. In a flash, your lighter's out. She hears the distinctive click of the metal and turns her head and ceases her own search. She reaches out and steadies your hand with hers. Because the flame stayed lit until you closed the cover, you didn't have to keep your finger pressed to the lever of the butane, as you needs to now, burning your fingertip. This also allowed you to hold the lighter with **GREATER ELEGANCE** and grace. She lights her cigarette, your eyes meet, she exhales heavenward. You close the lighter and open a new chapter in both your lives.

Maybe it was JFK's bare-headed appearance at his own inaugural that signaled the demise of men's hats in America. Before that, **MEN WORE HATS**. It was as simple as that. Not just policemen and firemen and cowboys, but the milkman, the guy in the ice cream truck, the cabby, the bus driver. Hats topped off your mufti. You didn't feel dressed without one. And even the **COMMON FEDORA**, standard attire for the working man, had a myriad of variations that allowed a man to make it his own. Whether he wanted his crown with a center crease, or a teardrop, or a **PORKPIE**

Whether there was a feather in his band. Whether he had a wide brim or narrow, what angle he turned it down, and if he

went with the grosgrain ribbing or left it plain. Like a baseball player's glove, a man's hat was very much his own.

Men have lost something from this era that goes beyond the toilet kit and sock garter and arrow-shaped tie clasp

designed to look like it's been shot through your tie. The time and care and **SENSE OF PLAY** that went into making

these items. The way they brought elements of craftsmanship and attention to detail into a man's life. Perhaps men today

could use an injection of some or all of those qualities. It could start with the shaving brush, which, right from the start,

gives the day a slower, more deliberate pace. And it could end with sitting in your special chair in the rumpus room,

SHOES OFF, SLIPPERS ON, SIPPING A COCKTAIL that you've just concocted with your own set of bar

equipment. And as soon as your wife or girlfriend gets home from work, she could take off her shoes

and join you.

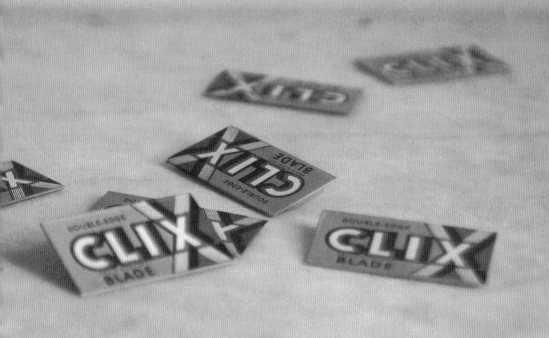

Most men do not know how to shave. Forget the models you see in shaving cream commercials. Sleek-chested, biceps glistening, stomachs rippled like challah breads, they jerk bladeless razors randomly across their faces with all the finesse of a snowmobile tearing through a stretch of Vermont woods. They look good, smell good, they get the girl, but they don't know squat about shaving.

The rhythm of a morning shave is a slow blues—a quiet, solitary, contemplative experience, like a pitcher's last moments in front of his locker before starting a big game.

It starts with wiping clear a circle of shower-fogged mirror just large enough to frame a face. The rest is left shrouded in mist. It's early yet. Who needs to see more of the world than is absolutely necessary.

Next, you wet your shaving brush with water slightly hotter than a cheek can stand. By the time you start lathering, it will be perfect. Start applying the soap at a spot just to the Jersey side of your chin, applying the lather in small, circular motions until the whiskers are covered. Once lathered, slide in a fresh blade, if necessary, and slip the old one into the slot in the back of the medicine cabinet, leaving it there to be pondered over by some twenty-first century archaeologist. The old double-edged razors with the thick, stainless steel handle, heavy as the fender on a '56 Caddie are preferred. Who needs a swivel-head razor? It took about a million years of

evolution to get our wrist as supple as it is, so why replace them.

The strokes of a good shave are smooth and steady. No quick jerks, no random tugs. Rushing a shave is like rushing a putt, a good cigar, or sex. Leave that to cherry-boy privates on their first weekend pass from Boot Camp. Let the weight of the razor do the work for you as you guide it with slow torque across the terrain of your cheek, the foothills of your neck, the dent in your chin.

A close shave ends with a splash of cool water, a towel, and a bit of balm to soothe your face. After all, your pores have taken a beating, your mug has been mugged, and it could use some soothing. But anything else, after shave, cologne, is superfluous, like spiking the ball after a touchdown.

There are some men who, no matter how careful they are, always wind up with a small cut. They can be spotted during the morning rush hour, a tell-tale piece of toilet paper stuck to their chin, dotted with blood in the center, like a miniature Japanese flag. Try as they might, these men can't avoid it. They just have a knack for nicks.

Shaving is one of the last bastions of manliness, more cloistered than the football field, the police force, garbage truck. Men shave. Women don't. It's our domain. And unless the winds from Three Mile Island and Chernobyl blew more ominously than we know, that's how it always will be.

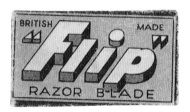

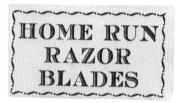

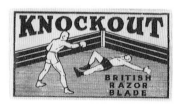

Blades were once packaged in paper and unwrapping them was very much a part of the morning shave. It was slightly dangerous—somewhat risky, and definitely the kind of thing that would impress a young boy watching his dad shave. It's how most men learn—just the two of you, alone together, doing something that mom definitely didn't do. You probably sat on the toilet seat, gazing up at the huge figure in his T-shirt, suspenders dangling at his side, hovering over the bathroom sink. Though there was joking at the start, like dabbing your cheek with the foamy shaving brush, once it was time to unwrap a fresh blade and put the razor into play, it was serious business. He made these odd faces—trying to kiss his ear or tuck his mouth into his chin, as he methodically and precisely executed his morning task.

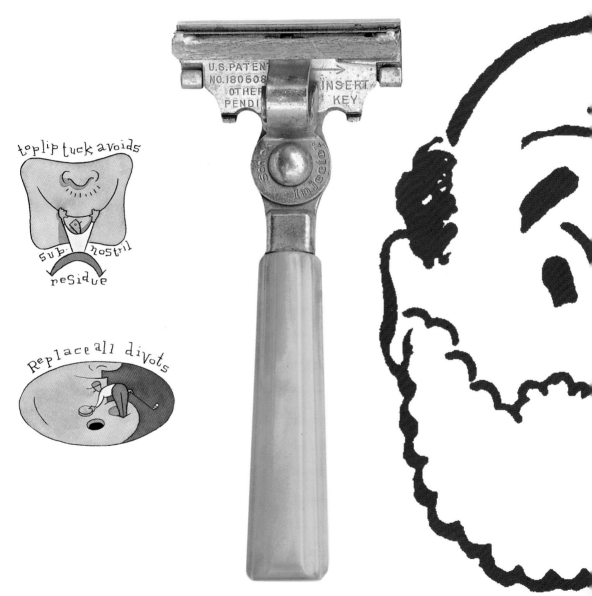

top lip tuck avoids

sub-nostril

residue

Replace all divots

U.S. PATENT
NO.180608
OTHER
PENDI
INSERT
KEY

Schick Injector

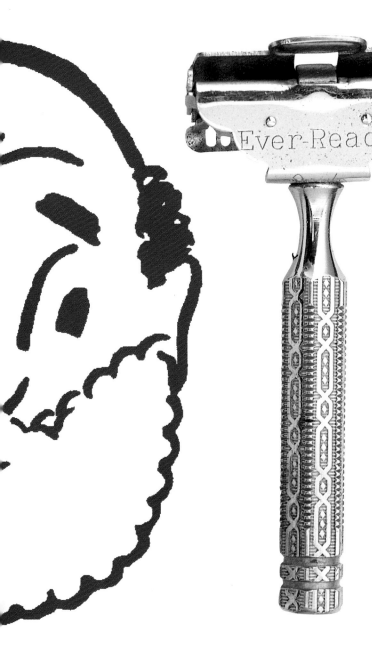

Ever-Ready

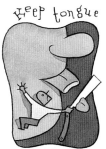

Keep tongue in mouth at all times

Shave with the grain to reduce blade resistance

LIKE A

Master Barber

Shave

SMOOTH - CLEAN - WET

You could be tall, dark, and handsome with swanky clothes and a hefty bankroll, but you'd never Get The Girl unless you chose the proper after shave.

After shaves and colognes spread your aura around, made you an irresistible engine of conquest. The sensuous scent turned women's heads, made them weak in the knees. They became like marionettes around you, with your after shave yanking the strings. Any female with nostrils caught in the Smell Impact Zone gets instantly sucked toward the Smell Source (you). You then choose which of the supplicants you wish to allow into your olfactory epicenter. This all has to happen in a matter of seconds, because the woman in question will soon be drawn in by the Smell Gravity of another orbiting Male Scent Vortex, becoming lost to you forever.

NEW
"Double-Action"
PALMOLIVE
After-Shave
Lotion

1. Cools Faster!

2. Soothes Longer!

ACTUALLY SOOTHES YOUR FACE FROM SHAVE TO SHAVE!

Girls were meant to be Gotten. They spent their waking hours primping themselves to be Gotten and their sleeping hours dreaming of the Prince who was going to Get them. Men only had to go about their business, making money, hitting each other, sticking cigars in their mouths. And, of course, charging up their Glance batteries to do some serious Getting. Because usually that's all it took to set the Getting wheels in motion. The Big Glance. Glance properly, your Glancee was Gotten. Once Gotten, she was yours, and you'd better know what to do with her. Men suffering from Weak Glance had to employ Glance Enhancers, such as Brylcream or skinny ties to look taller. Then, with Glance enhanced, they hit the streets to do some serious Getting while the getting was good.

You want nothing in your medicine chest except the basics. Like shaving talc. Soothing and slightly scented, it keeps face and neck dry on hot days. But just in case your paramour starts snooping around the bathroom while ostensibly powdering her nose, any penicillin, fungus medication, or regularity encouragement should be immediately removed.

Don't be a "poor fish"— be her dream man!

Octopus He combs his hair with water. After water dries, his hair sticks out and hangs down like tentacles. Kreml Hair Tonic keeps hair neatly in place from morn 'til night.

Eel Often called a "heel" by the ladies. He plasters his hair down with grease. Looks just like a gigolo. Kreml keeps hair handsomely groomed yet never leaves it looking oily or greasy.

Speckled Trout Specks look beautiful on a trout but *not* dandruff specks on your shoulders. Kreml is famous to remove dandruff flakes. Leaves scalp feeling and looking *so clean.*

"He man" and "Head man"

Will her **caress test** tell tales about your hair?

MENNEN
Cream Hair Oil
KEEPS YOUR HAIR NEATLY IN PLACE
CONTAINS LANOLIN
NON-ALCOHOLIC NET 5 FL. OZ.

20% more
Cream Hair Oil
for your money!

Grooms hair, never greases it

The proof is in the palm of your hand!

When she runs her fingers lightly through your hair, will you pass the test? Try

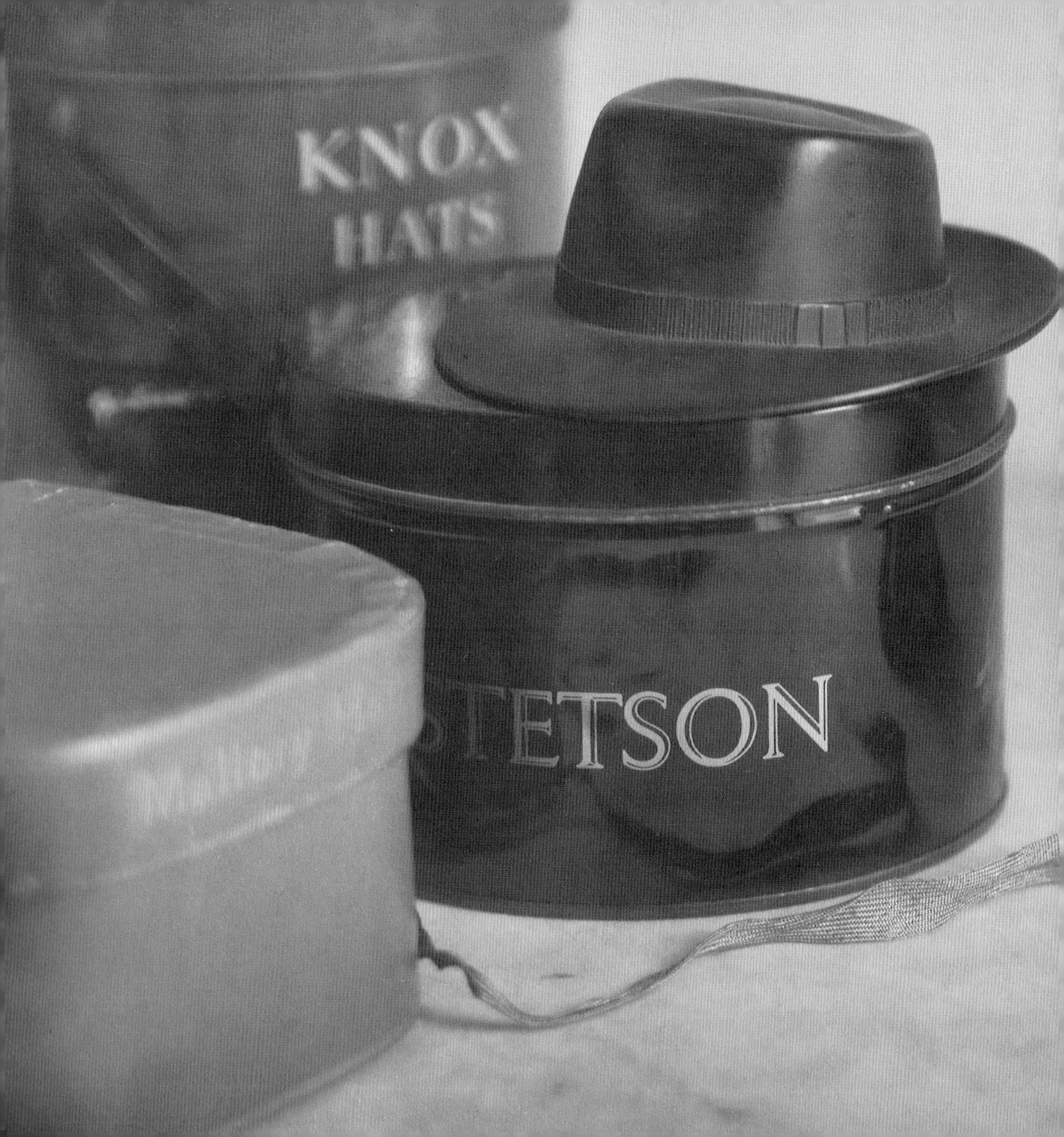
KNOX
HATS
STETSON

Time was a man didn't leave the house without his hat. Adjusting the crease in the crown as he headed out the door, he donned it at his signature angle, fixing the brim so it was just right. Only then was he ready to face the city, join the other hats, a sea swell of bowlers, fedoras, porkpies, and tweed caps emerging from the subway. Decades are marked by changing brim-sizes. When Hollywood wants to evoke a past era, they turn first to cars and hats.

Who would Bogart be without his fedora, brim bent down, shadowing his face. Or Huntz Hall, poet laureate of the Dead End, without his beanie, made from some discarded gray Homborg, the brim ripped off, folded over, and then cut into a crown. Sam Snead couldn't sink a three-foot putt without his hat. Tails weren't enough for Fred Astaire— he needed the top hat, too. And Mrs. Kalabash would never have drifted into sleep, if Jimmy Durante wasn't clutching his hat to his heart, wherever she was.

From Robin Hood, with his green felt with feather, through Dean Martin with his narrow-brimmed Dorset, men have worn hats. Home was where you hung it. It was what you tipped to acknowledge a pair of silk-hosed gams walking past; what your mistress tossed on the divan before letting you know how long it seemed since your last visit; what was passed for collection after the *spiel* at the local Mission; what you held over your heart as the Anthem played before the ball game.

That "the hat made the man" was a given. Bowlers headed to corner offices on Wall Street; stove-pipes to the opera; gray fedoras worked hard and watched their annuities grow; wool stevedore caps went stevedoring; Red Caps towed luggage; yellow ones drove Checkers; white caps delivered milk; Greenwich Village bohemians donned berets; soda jerks saluted their jerk-ness in white paper caps.

Dad's hat hanging on the hook in the front hall meant he was home. And who could resist the urge to try it on, the brim down to your nose where you took the heady smell of sweat, leather, and Vitalis. Your dad's smell. Unmistakable.

Fingerprints could give you his name, but the way a man wore his hat could tell you his whole story. Was it pulled down low, sullenly locking out the world; or tilted back, to give a wink to any passing fancy. Did it still have the haberdasher's creases, or was the crown now distinctly marked with your personality. Was it starting to fray at the edges, the felt showing signs of too many unexpected rainstorms; or was it fresh, crisp, newly blocked. Did it smell of sweat or fish? Was it dark with soot from fixing the boiler or speckled greenish white with sea gull shit after a day loading ships at the docks?

If a hat you were trying on was too small, it fit you *too soon*. If it was too large, and sunk down to the bridge of your nose, you were suddenly a kid again, playing in the living room, because the first thing you did when you were impersonating your dad was to put on his hat.

make eye contact

effect 3-point grip

tip the hat

post-doff swivel & glance

27

HATS MAKE THE MAN

Hats weren't worn just for style—they identified what a man did. At work, it never came off, becoming practically a part of his head. The milkman always had his white hat on while he was delivering his pints and quarts. The visor wasn't long enough to shade him from the sun, so he must have worn it for another reason— perhaps simply because he was the milkman. And the only time he took off his hat was to hang it on your bed post. Beatniks, whose work it was to avoid work, always kept their berets on, lest anyone think they needed gainful employment. And hats could be expressive. The policeman with his hat tilted back, scratching his head, him you could get to overlook that stop sign you didn't see. But that other cop, with the visor pulled down low, he's going to throw the book at you.

Not as much of an oxymoron as you would think. Who do you think read Mailer, James T. Farrell, Nelson Algren, James Jones, Hemingway, O'Hara, Runyon? Algren's *Never Come, Morning* is a torrid, dense novel about a young Polish boxer trying to make it in the big time but never able to leave behind his desperate past. A tough read, it sold 950,000 copies in paperback. And that wasn't Algren's best seller.

The lurid cover might have helped, but every paperback had a lurid cover back then. Faulkner got cleavage on his paperbacks. Pouty lips. A suggestion of bondage. So did Flaubert. Some deserved the full-tilt licentious boogie on the cover—whips and bondage or B-girls in a doorway half lit by street lamps, a cigarette between their lips. James M. Cain's novels earned those covers. Likewise, Jim Thompson's, all paperback originals. And when the backs of their books screamed out tags like "torrid," "racy," "electric," "she didn't know what she wanted until it was too late," they didn't let you down.

The most literate, widely read sports writers used metaphors far beyond the realm of sports. Their interest in the larger picture was keen. Jimmy Cannon left the daily routine of his sports column to become one of the most esteemed reporters covering W.W.II and Korea. A.J. Leibling wrote about boxing and gourmet cooking. And when Red Smith wrote a eulogy for a passing sportsman, it rivaled in thought and feeling any essay by any of the "literary" types of the period. Turf-wise New Yorkers recall with reverence the *Daily Telegraph*, known in racetrack parlance as "The Telly," whose reportage of world and local news, though brief, was literate and in-depth.

Men's magazines were not the fatuous affairs they are now, indistinguishable from the women's rags. *Esquire* was large, elegant, very sophisticated, and devoted to jazz and an intellectual view of sports. The stories and humor it published were of the highest caliber. The same with *Playboy*, whose early forays into nudity were usually sidelong peeks, never full-frontal views.

Jazz music was a big part of a man's world. Hipsters first dug Harlem Stride and Kansas City Jump, then later Bop and Cool. Their dress and lingo reflected their passion for the music. Anything from a zoot suit with the reet pleat to berets and shades like Diz and Monk. Men's magazines covered the jazz scene in depth. Annual readers' polls were a feature of *Esquire*, and the results were actually of some consequence to the winners. While the Dolls kept up with the latest Hollywood gossip, the Guys read Leonard Feather and Rudi Blesh and Nat Hentoff to keep abreast of Satchmo and Pres and Zoot and all the latest musical developments.

The jazz club was another spot where men hung out. College kids, financiers, and sailors on shore leave rubbed elbows in smoky basement rooms where beer and music flowed freely. Jazz cut across all social boundaries. Blacks and whites mixed freely in the smaller clubs, at least up North. And Teddy Wilson broke the color barrier in music many years before baseball saw the light.

GENTLER

Nº4 Fall 1951

THE LARGEST SELLING FIFTY CENT MAGAZINE IN THE WORLD · THIS PRINTING $50,000

Esquire

· THE MAGAZINE FOR MEN ·

FICTION · SPORTS · HUMOR
CLOTHES · ART · CARTOONS

PRICE FIFTY CENTS
CANADIAN PRICE FIFTY-FIVE CENTS

---

flair

All Male Is

July 1950
Fifty cents

HUNTING and FISHING 5¢

PLEASURE

MAGAZINE

First Edition

$5,000
PRIZE

TRAVEL · ENTERTAINMENT · SPORTS
FICTION · CARTOONS · FASHIONS

THE Gent

AN APPROACH TO RELAXATION

THE GENT'S JAZZ AMERICA

BURTON WOHL
ROBERT BLOCH

The cover's anything but cute. A glimpse into the dark side, the seamy underworld of the soul. Norman Rockwell ripped inside out. Good girls gone bad. Bad girls gone worse. Books to open like switchblades. The sordid scene on the cover, the black-gloved hand holding the ice pick piercing the creamy white bosom, ensured no one on the bus home after work will mistake you for a Commie intellectual subversive. No way. This is a *man's* book you're reading.

MASKED . . . she watched a killer strike. The mystery woman was the only witness. But would her abandoned behavior keep her from talking?

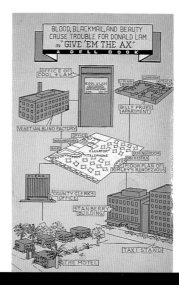

BLOOD, BLACKMAIL, AND BEAUTY CAUSE TROUBLE FOR DONALD LAM IN "GIVE 'EM THE AX"

"TORRID!"

"TENSE!"

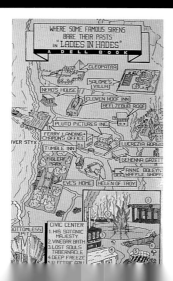

WHERE SOME FAMOUS SIRENS BARE THEIR PASTS IN "LADIES IN HADES"

POPIN'S PLACE SCENE OF A MURDER IN "THE BLACKBIRDER"

BRENT HOUSE AT BALIFOLD SCENE OF MURDERS IN "WOLF IN MAN'S CLOTHING"

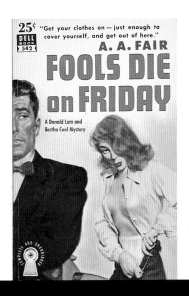

25¢

DELL BOOK 542

"Get your clothes on — just enough to cover yourself, and get out of here."

A. A. FAIR
FOOLS DIE on FRIDAY

A Donald Lam and Bertha Cool Mystery

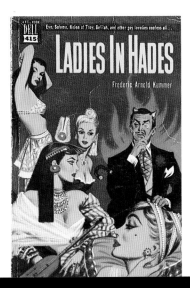

A DELL BOOK 415

Eve, Salome, Helen of Troy, Delilah, and other gay lovelies confess all...

LADIES IN HADES

Frederic Arnold Kummer

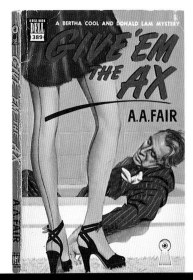

A DELL BOOK 389

A BERTHA COOL AND DONALD LAM MYSTERY

GIVE 'EM THE AX

A.A. FAIR

"LUSTY!"   "HIGH-VOLTAGE!"   "SPECTACULAR!"

GENTLEMEN AREN'T SISSIES

A Modern Guidebook for the Young Man About Town Who Wants to Know His Way Around

By Norton Hughes Jonathan

Illustrated by Palacio Dave

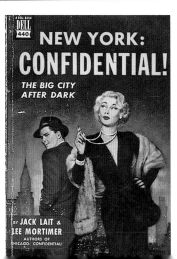

DELL BOOK 440

NEW YORK: CONFIDENTIAL!

THE BIG CITY AFTER DARK

By JACK LAIT & LEE MORTIMER

AUTHORS OF CHICAGO: CONFIDENTIAL!

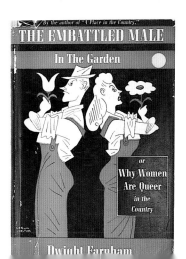

By the author of "A Place in the Country,"

THE EMBATTLED MALE

In The Garden

or
Why Women
Are Queer
in the
Country

Dwight Fareham

LPs

With the rise of the LP there emerged a new sound that existed only on record. Mood Music. Part lush jazz, part anthem for the narcoleptic, these were standards played as no one ever had before. They were meant to set The Mood— to bewitch and intoxicate. For further enticement, the women on the album covers were sultry and sophisticated, in low-cut evening gowns, a cocktail held in an elbow-length black glove, leaning forward, as if all they needed were the sound of muted trumpet and aching violins to tip them on to your couch. Stack an inch of platters on the tall spindle of your High Fidelity Hi-Fi, fill your cocktail shaker with the juice of two Manhattans, and snuggle up with your filly to dig the Hi-Fonic, Full Color, 360 Degree, 3-D Sound that will send you straight to Moodsville.

KEY CASE

Back when trousers were cut wide and had roomy pockets, you didn't want your keys jangling as you walked, accenting each step like Buddy Rich riding his top hat.

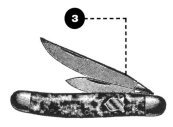

POCKET KNIFE

It was, at most, two blades, one long, one short, for cutting twine-wrapped packages or that hunk of salami in your lunchbox, and facilitating some minor repairs while impressing any wife, kids, or fair maidens in the vicinity.

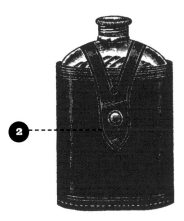

FLASK

If thin, it rode on your hip and held only a few surreptitious swigs. Larger ones fit in the breast pocket of your overcoat and carried sufficient fluid to spike a large bowl of punch.

RABBIT'S FOOT

An American boy's mojo, it was one of those mysterious childhood icons, like a fungo bat, caps, Bazooka Joe, whoopee cushions, and the cardboard caddy around a Howard Johnson's hot dog.

POCKETS

Pockets are a man's domain, holding your essential equipment—wallet, keys, cash, stiletto, lucky charm, lighter, lint. Wear your jeans often enough, white patches emerge, outlining your wallet, keys, and favorite Zippo. Pockets protect and hide what's yours. Magicians load secret pockets with a fabulous array of objects. Cops rely on back pockets to keep their logbooks and flashlights. Spies and PIs pack them with jimmies, mini-cameras, decoders, and other tools of the trade. As you age, the contents of your pockets age with you. Shakespeare's melancholy Jacques could have used them to chart the stages of man. In youth, slingshots and baseball cards. Later, a jackknife, latch key, and rabbit's foot. As a teenager, a pack of humps, dice, a rubber, and a solitary finsky. In adulthood, wallet, lighter, and car keys. Finally, a bile-soaked handkerchief and little container of pills.

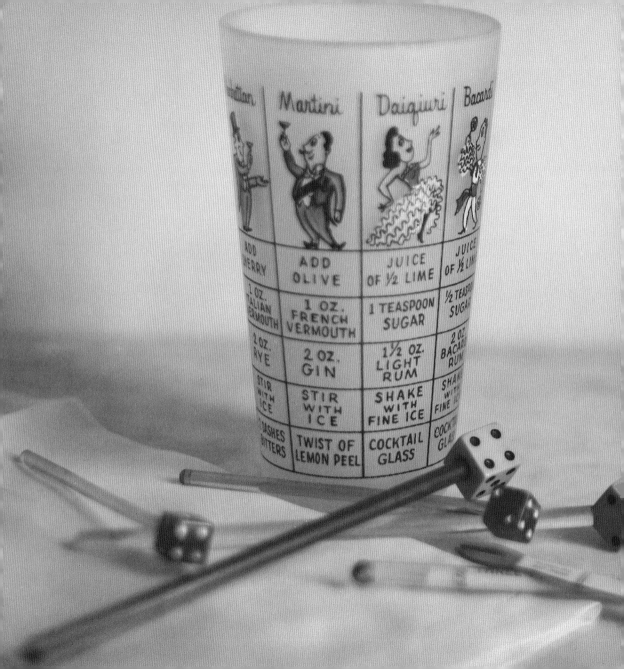

Y ou and the Mrs. are having a dinner party. On the coffee table, the cocktail platter is ready, cubicles filled with party snacks—chips, mixed nuts, Ritz crackers, thin pretzels, celery and carrot sticks surrounding a bowl of your wife's famous secret-recipe dip. You fit the long spindle into the hi-fi and arrange a stack of 10 inch LPs—Frank Sinatra, Sarah Vaughn, Chet Baker, Dean Martin.

The doorbell rings—ding-dong. (This was when doorbells actually went "ding-dong"—dogs barked "woof-woof" and "ruff"—people stubbed toes and said "ouch.") Ding-dong. Your friends are here! Three other couples—Buddy and Doris, Hank and Phyllis, Barney and Marge. Hand shakes, cheek-pecks, back slaps all around. Buddy brought some Cherry Heering for after dinner. Phyllis made a chopped liver mold in the shape of a football. And Marge presented a large tin of bridge mix which Bunny (your wife) claimed "we wouldn't finish in a million years." Barney muttered that "he told her it was too big." "Shush," Marge said and slapped his arm.

Greetings over, you all disperse from the foyer. The women go into the kitchen, where Bunny has to put her signature dish "Steak in a Bag" into the oven so you can eat in a half hour.

The men retire to . . . where else?

The Bar.

Unlike Barney, who built his bar into the paneled wall of his basement Rumpus Room, yours is in the den. It's a mahogany affair, with a metal sculpture of the venerable Happy Drunk leaning against a lamppost adorning the front. The three stools and the padded bumper lining the bar are covered with leopard Naugahyde. The classic jungle motif.

The inside of the bar is lined with shelves that house the bar ware. When it comes to high-precision equipment, the Manhattan Project has nothing on you and your bar. You have a perfectly calibrated jigger; a double-action stirrer to give you gyroscopic rotation as you stir; the liquor bottles are capped with streamlined stainless steel pourers, which produce a clean, steady stream for easy measuring and create a majestic silver sky-line on the shelf, like the Chrysler and Empire State buildings; there's also an assortment of shakers, strainers, church key openers (for beer and mixers), two kinds of ice crushers—a hammer and bag affair and a large heavy glass fitted with a quadri-flanged plunger which breaks up the cubes quite neatly; and your special bar knife for cutting limes and lemon twists which no one else is allowed to use (meaning your wife).

Behind the bar, on several rows of glass shelves, are your glasses. You have six different sets, which enable you to serve most every drink, including martinis, Manhattans, Tom Collins, straight shots (how boring), beer, and after-dinner cordials in their appropriate glasses. Barney (because he has to have everything) has those tall, thin glasses for the exotic Hawaiian drinks he likes to make and even the paper umbrellas and stirrers adorned with native girls in hula skirts.

Dino's lilting baritone grows louder as the girls join you in the den. You whip them up a quick batch of strawberry daiquiris and build another round for your pals. Marge reads one of the slightly naughty quips on the cocktail napkin and the laughter is general.

"Cheers," shouts Barney, his mouth full of bridge mix. "Cheers!"

Hubba-hubba. The evening's off to a great start. Everything's just hunky-dory.

Here's a wedding present you didn't wait to receive by chance. This one was from jump street—was the first thing in the bag packed for the honeymoon (along with the stuff from the pharmacy). The judge certified your wedding, this mini-shaker and glass set validated it—made it real—the trinity that is your marriage. Yours. Mine. Ours.

With The Falls outside your Honeymoon suite (the first suite *you* ever stayed in), you re-lock the door after charging down the hall in your boxers to fill the ice bucket (while *she,* the little pip, locked you out, hoping the old biddies next door would catch you in your skivvies). Once inside, you settle down to mix the biggest drink of your life—A Prelude to the Nuptializing. The missus—jeez, *your* missus—is in her negligee, looking ravishing in the crepuscule. You shake the shaker to hide your shaking. You pour. You touch glasses. "Cheers, Babydoll. Here's to us."

Two basic drinking motifs on these shakers, pink elephants and hopping jazz rhythms, just right for a jubilant crowd—for pouring drinks to the beat of Louis Prima with a lampshade on your head. The jolly elephants will meet you later, when you're supine on the divan, and will tuck you in for the night. The stirrers are slightly more refined—images of golf and elegant suppers; a touch of whimsy with the mermaid and tipsy seahorse; and a whistle, in case you over imbibe on New Year's Eve, so someone can blow it on you.

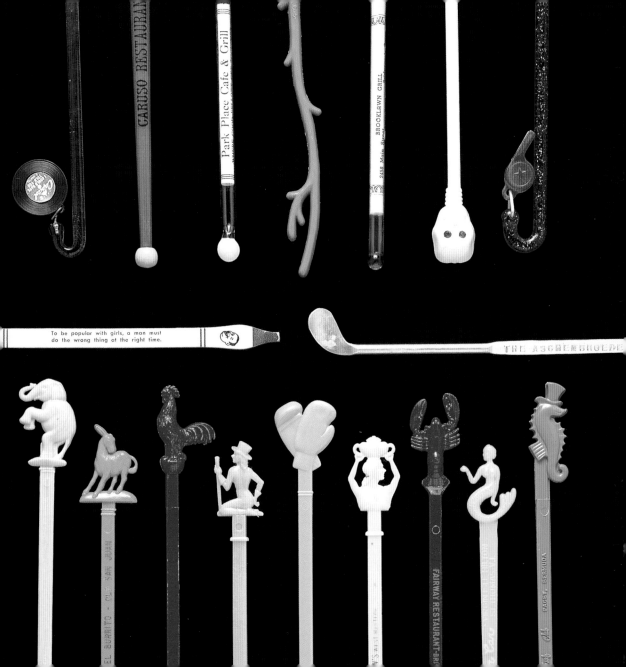

CARUSO RESTAURANT

Park Place Cafe & Grill

BROOKLAWN GRILL

2458 Main Street

To be popular with girls, a man must do the wrong thing at the right time.

THE ASCHENBRÖDEL

EL BURRITO - CLE SAN JUAN

FAIRWAY RESTAURANT

The portable bullet shot glass—Mutt to your hip-flask's Jeff. Fortifying, giving comfort to you and three friends in the frigid stands at football Homecoming or huddled in the front hedges of a Newport mansion, working up the courage to crash the party.

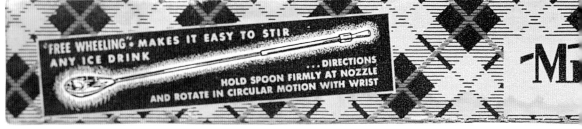

The Jigger Whack was everything a man needed to crush ice. Fill the canvas bag with cubes, close it up, and whack it with the whacker. Use the jigger to scoop out one drink's worth of expertly crushed ice. It was also a perfect conversation starter. "Could you show me how you Jigger Whack?" And once again, it breaks the ice.

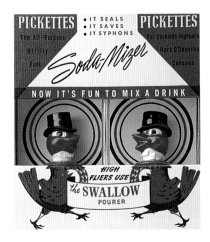

OWNERS No 1082   REGISTERED AT
MAY'S
1314 & 1114
ATLANTIC AVE.

YOU PAY

PIEL'S BEER
ERNEST JAMBOR
INC.
1202 WALNUT ST.
PHILADELPHIA

ar Swivel

Another Member of the
Mr. Bartender PRODUCTS
LOS ANGELES, CALIFORNIA   PATENT PENDING

WHITTEN MOTOR VEHICLE CO.
ABBOTT-DETROIT, BRUSH &
OAKLAND MOTOR CARS
152 WASHINGTON ST.
PROV.   R. I.

DRINK
SHEERTOWN
BEVERAGES

49

Mr. Tipsy was the king, and your best bottle of Scotch his throne. He lorded there, his own jester, merrily dispensing joy and wisdom one jigger at a time. Late at night, when the house is quiet, and not a creature is stirring, not even a mouse, Mr. Tipsy was happy to keep you company. When no one else was, *he'd* be there for you. Push down on his hat and out of his nose came a soothing dram. He never slept, he just got happier and happier. He was a corker, that Mr. Tipsy. And he knew that when the well ran dry, you'd get him a new home. And that made him happier still.

De Luxe
FOUR KINGS

ONE QUART — 90 PROOF

TRADE MARK

BLENDED WHISKEY

BLENDED AND BOTTLED BY
KASKO DISTILLERS PRODUCTS CORP.
PHILADELPHIA, PA.
©1935

HALF PINT — 90 PROOF

Red Circle

STRAIGHT BOURBON WHISKEY

BOTTLED BY
E. Kahn & Co., Inc.
BALTIMORE, MD.
6-13

95 PROOF — 1 FULL QT

100% MARYLAND STRAIGHT RYE

CARROLL CLUB WHISKEY

BOTTLED FOR
THE CARROLL CO.
1636 WALNUT STREET PHILADELPHIA PA.
PA. LIC-1-41

MORONEY

ARMY AND NAVY

BRAND
REG. U. S. PAT. OFF.

A BLEND OF
STRAIGHT RYE WHISKIES
• • •

BOTTLED AT THE DISTILLERY
FOR
JAMES MORONEY
PHILADELPHIA, PA., U. S. A.
ESTABLISHED 1845
LICENSE PA. 1-16

my FRIEND

ONE QUART — 90 PROOF
TRADE MARK

STRAIGHT WHISKEY

BOTTLED BY
KASKO DISTILLERS PRODUCTS CORP.
PHILADELPHIA, PA.
©1935

G·O·TAYLOR

Blended Whiskey

90 PROOF — 1 QUART

Blended and Bottled by
C. H. GRAVES & SONS CO.
Distillers since 1849
BOSTON
Chester H. Graves & Sons
GENUINE BEARS OUR SIGNATURE
M-18

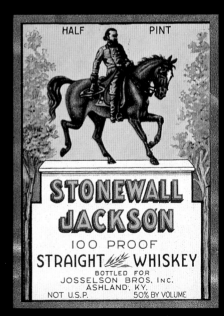

HALF PINT

STONEWALL JACKSON

100 PROOF
STRAIGHT WHISKEY

BOTTLED FOR
JOSSELSON BROS. INC.
ASHLAND, KY.
NOT U.S.P. — 50% BY VOLUME

Harpo's Special

What's It?

Arise My Love

Marconi Wire Less

Prairie Chicken

Ward 8

THE RECIPES

This was the time when comedians didn't improvise—they told jokes, the same ones each night. The same was true for building drinks, which was in no way an impromptu undertaking. The recipes were clearly established. The exact proportions for everything from a Doolittle Special to a Diki-diki to a Connecticut Bullfrog were worked out to the half-ounce by master bartenders from exotic locales like The Savoy, The Algonquin Hotel, and Delmonico's. And while the wife had the burden of searching through her cookbooks for her recipes, yours are conveniently printed on the side of the shakers, glasses, cocktail napkins, and, for good measure, on the bottom of the serving platter. There was also the "Bartender's Guide" for quick reference and inspiration.

If poker players nixed the diamond pinkie rings and had, in general, better couture, the great ones would be recognized for the National Treasures they are. They share many of the same skills as great novelists, like Dickens. Because poker is not one hand, but many chapters and many characters. Like in Dickens, one tiny detail in the opening (a twitch, say, when an opponent's bluffing; how he grips the cards tighter when he has a good hand) may have monumental significance at the dénouement, when the stakes are highest.

And a true poker player knows more about the human psyche than any psychiatrist. Because psychiatrists rarely see their patients in action, only *hear* reports about specific behavior (and the philosopher Wittgenstein long ago laid to rest any hope that *language* is of any use to us when we're trying to communicate something important). Poker players observe *behavior;* deduce patterns of behavior in their opponents that their opponents themselves are not aware of.

To see if you have the poker player's acumen, try this simple test. Give a friend a coin, have him put his hands behind his back, then bring out his fists, the coin hidden in one of them. The odds are even money you'll find the coin the first time. After that, however, you should be able to assess his behavior, to *know.* Will he change hands to fool you? If he thinks *you* think he will change hands, will he stand pat? It's up to you to psyche him out. To use all your guile and insight. Pick the hand with the coin eight times in a row and you're ready to win some money at the poker table.

The Ponies. It was once the sport of kings. Winners were chosen not just from past performance, but by how they looked in the paddock—lather on the neck, possibly a sign of nervousness; extra tape on the ankles, possibly favoring that leg. Starlets draped over the arms of rich producers would point out the ones they liked, those with a deep chestnut coat, or an aura of strength. And their mogul paramours would then put down a C-note on that horse to Show.

But except for the big stakes races, horse racing is now relegated primarily to life's stragglers—busboys with the afternoon off, retired civil servants, taxi drivers killing time before their shifts start. Only at tracks like Saratoga or Santa Anita has it retained some of its glamour. Producers still consult their high-priced tip sheets, though now they simultaneously cut deals on their cellular phones and chomp on Havanas that cost ten bucks instead of ten cents, because these days they have to be smuggled in through Canada.

In the world of the great sportswriters—Grantland Rice, Jimmy Cannon, Red Smith, the track was as much a part of their beat as the gridiron, the diamond, the links, the hardwood, or the ring. They would talk about a horse's courage, its fight. How it battled for the lead down the stretch and wouldn't quit. How it ran like a champion. As if the horse *knew.* As if horses were any other proud, spirited athlete. And if you go to the track, and see the horses live, hear them thunder down the stretch, the 12-1 shot you picked holding off the favorite, you'll swear too that courage and heart and pride are what motivate a thoroughbred.

1 If a horse has come in second or third in his last few races, beware. Don't assume it's now ready to be a winner. It may simply be a second place horse.

2 If a horse that was ridden by a weak jockey the previous race now has one of the premier jockeys on him, it may be a sign that the trainer is getting more serious about the horse's prospects.

3 Beware of horses that are changing distances, especially sprinters moving to longer races. Unused to the distance, they may tire before the home stretch.

4 More important than what position the horse finished in his previous races is which horses beat him in those races. Coming in fourth behind three highly regarded stakes horses may not be so disgraceful. If the horse is not running in such distinguished company now, he may be a good bet.

5 Most horses who win races do so within 14 days of their last race. Horses with longer layoffs should be shied away from, unless the horse has a premier trainer, who may know exactly what he's doing.

6 If you're in line at the window and standing directly behind a gentleman of Oriental heritage, always bet what he's betting.

7 And, above all, keep in mind what Damon Runyon said, "All horseplayers die broke."

Big Tiger

Little Dog

Monkey Flush

Runt

POKER TIPS

Embrace your solitude, because playing poker is a solitary experience—you against the rest of the table. But don't forget to laugh if anyone says anything funny. Otherwise you won't be invited back.

♠

Be patient. Do not give in to the urge to "see what happens."

♣

Be prepared to back your solid hands to the limit like a running back hitting an open hole in the line.

♦

Never draw to an inside straight.

♥

At some point in the first hour, throw a bluff. This establishes you as someone who knows how to bluff and will help confuse your opponents later in the game.

♠

Three deuces beats any two pairs.

♣

Never play catch-up poker. You will just lose faster.

♦

The only way to win is to not be afraid to fold. You always have a right to fold, even after you've won a big pot.

♥

Watch that you don't eat too many potato chips—the grease can make the cards slip out of your hand.

RULES
OF
PINOCHLE

Out of the tenements and other urban centers around the country emerged an eccentric hybrid of bridge and gin called pinochle. It's fast and vicious and is played with that *other* deck, the one with two sets of picture cards, aces, nines, and tens. Three guys play. With four, one sits out but all add to the pot. Deal 15 cards to each player and 3 in the kitty. The guy that takes the bid calls trump and replaces the kitty with 3 from his hand. The other two players then try to stop him. Pinochle was played during lunch in the Garment Center, between takes in Hollywood, in hotel lobbies among travelling salesmen, by grifters on the lam listening to reports of their capers on the radio, in the steam bath lounge with a cheese danish and a glass of tea for refreshment.

THIS WALLET HAS 8 EXCLUSIVE FEATURES EVERY MAN WILL LIKE

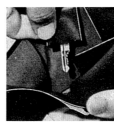

1. SECRET POCKET. Large bills concealed behind a flap that looks exactly like the lining. No need to expose money in public places. *This feature is patented.*

2. DUPLICATE KEY POCKET. This concealed pocket for emergency keys prevents "locked-out" accidents.

3. SLIDING CARD POCKET. Just a pull of the tab brings cards, identification, etc. into view instantly.

Be Sure to See the New Patented Amity "Director" Key Kaddy

4. FREE REGISTRATION. Thousands of billfolds and Key Kaddies found and returned to their owners every year.

ALSO: (6) Sliding Stay, to prevent bulkiness; (7) Branded genuine top-grain leathers; (8) Edges turned and stitched for thin construction and longer wear.

5. CARD FILE. Cards kept clean and easy to identify by different-colored transparent celluloid covers. Cards can't spill out.

You remove keys *individually* . . . quickly and easily . . . and with no danger of others spilling from the new patented Amity "Director" removable hook Key Kaddy. Available in matched sets with "Director" billfolds, or individually at $1.50 and up.

One of the few things that the thought of replacing leaves you distinctly unsettled. That's the curve of *your* buttocks it's shaped to, *your* receipts and paper scraps puffing it out to almost bursting, a bit of your soul rubbed into the leather. You've broken it in, the leather worn down in spots by the particular way you pry it out of your pocket. Its smell, distinct. Its patina, an extension of your dermis.

There's a shiny new one buried in your top drawer, a birthday gift from an aging aunt. But you can't bring yourself to draft it into service. The one you have has a few more good years left. Yeah, just a few.

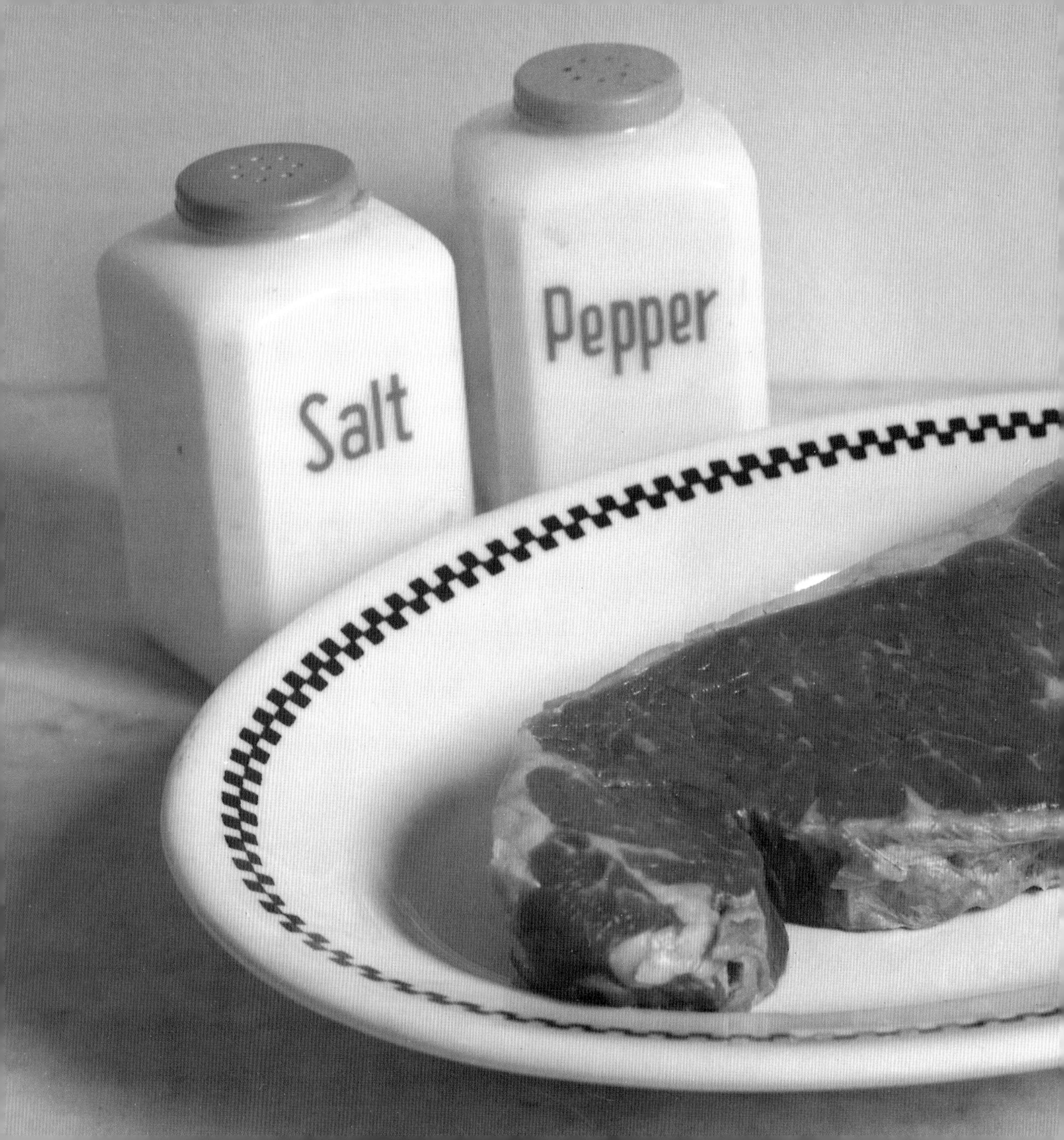
Salt
Pepper

BLUE PLATE

"**Hi** Honey, I'm home."

The male suburbanite's mantra. I'm home, I'm hungry, I want my dinner.

A man's gotta eat, but he's not gonna cook, not gonna set foot in the kitchen, except to pop a beer and cut enough salami to stay him until supper. Because the kitchen just ain't his domain. He could have been under a hood all day, fixing the piston rings on a flathead Ford; or in the operating room, performing a spinal tap on a kid who had a relapse of the mumps; or running the controls on a sixty foot crane—all delicate and painstaking jobs, requiring great skill and dexterity. But enter the kitchen, to be confronted with actually lifting a pan or slicing an onion or filling a pot with water, and he loses control of his major muscles, his coordination disappears, the laws of physics cease to function, and he winds up standing helplessly in the center of the linoleum.

The one wrinkle, the one culinary ace up his sleeve, was breakfast. Fingers to his lips, he wakes the kids on Saturday morning and quietly leads them tiptoeing downstairs for Saturday breakfast. "Whataya say, kids? We'll let Mom sleep. I'll make you guys some pancakes."

Out from the deepest recesses of the cabinetry emerge pots and pans that have not seen the light of day since the wedding shower. Bowls crusty with dust get a quick rinse. Because every piece of heavy equipment is needed for this invasion. All the big guns. No paltry European-style breakfast this. *Dad's* making a meal *his* way. And soon the Formica is littered with broken egg shells, globs of flour and milk now hardened into glue, half-filled measuring cups and spoons, a Gypsy-family of bowls and pans and pots and somehow, in the one frying pan that made it to the stove, are gathered a small confederacy of pancakes, waiting to be flipped and served to the adoring, awestruck progeny. And when, later that morning, the wife looks slack-jawed at the carnage in her kitchen, you can say "Morning Honey, did you get some rest?"

Though wives rule the kitchen, the Man lords over the grill. The Grill.

The very words rev the taste buds to thunderous RPMs.

But barbecuing is no casual affair. It is fraught with intrigue, secret techniques for lighting the coals, for quelling flare-ups, for evening the heat. It is, in fact, a sacred undertaking. Like a Crusade. Your goal, The Holy Grill. And you, High Priest of the charcoal. The backyard is your temple, the grill itself, a sacrificial altar to hundreds of steaks, burgers, hot dogs, chicken breasts—anointed with barbecue sauce or Teriyaki; the long spatula, your scepter; the apron, your vestment, emblazoned with the mythopoeic iconography— "Genius At Work."

Because if you have the grill, it means you have a backyard. And a backyard means you've arrived, that you're of the landed gentry. That week in steerage one or two generations back, the long, ghastly trip from Palermo or Poland or Austria or Ireland was not spent in vain. Because that's *your* patio furniture baking in the sun, your sprinkler whirling like a Dervish in the center of the lawn, your kids playing on the swingset, your wife winding the Brownie 8mm camera, about to permanently capture you all for jerky, spastic cinematic prosperity.

GRILL WORK

It's Saturday afternoon and Dad's taking care of dinner. Look at the joy beaming from Mom's face. She knows what's coming next. The table's set, the punch all made. His daughter's tricycle and croquet set lie idle, forgotten, overshadowed by the anticipation she must feel for the perfectly grilled steak her dad is about to serve her. And look at that grill. He built that! Himself! Probably following the plans in *Popular Mechanics*. Dad's Big Grill. Something to show off to dinner guests—even in winter, the chimney protruding through the snow. "Nice job, Gil. I could go for one of those T-bones right now."

Men like sandwiches—both making them and eating them. Like painting by numbers, it's easy to feel you're expressing yourself, piling on the cold cuts and sliced cheese, cole slaw, pickles, lettuce, tomatoes, mayo and mustard. The bigger it is, the more precariously balanced, the more they feel like an expert craftsman.

© King Features Syndicate, Inc.

THE BIG APRON

Barbecue tools are big, oversized, manly, and rugged. Nothing dainty or frilly about this equipment. After you finish flipping the steaks, you can use the spatula to clear a stump from the backyard. The apron is big and brawny and hangs down almost to your ankles. It has a cute saying, corny by design, to let the world know this isn't your usual attire— that it's only for this occasion that you wear an apron, like the festooned costumes at Mardis Gras. And the platter, big as a garbage can cover, to hold steaks that would choke a Tyrannosaurus.

MR FIX IT

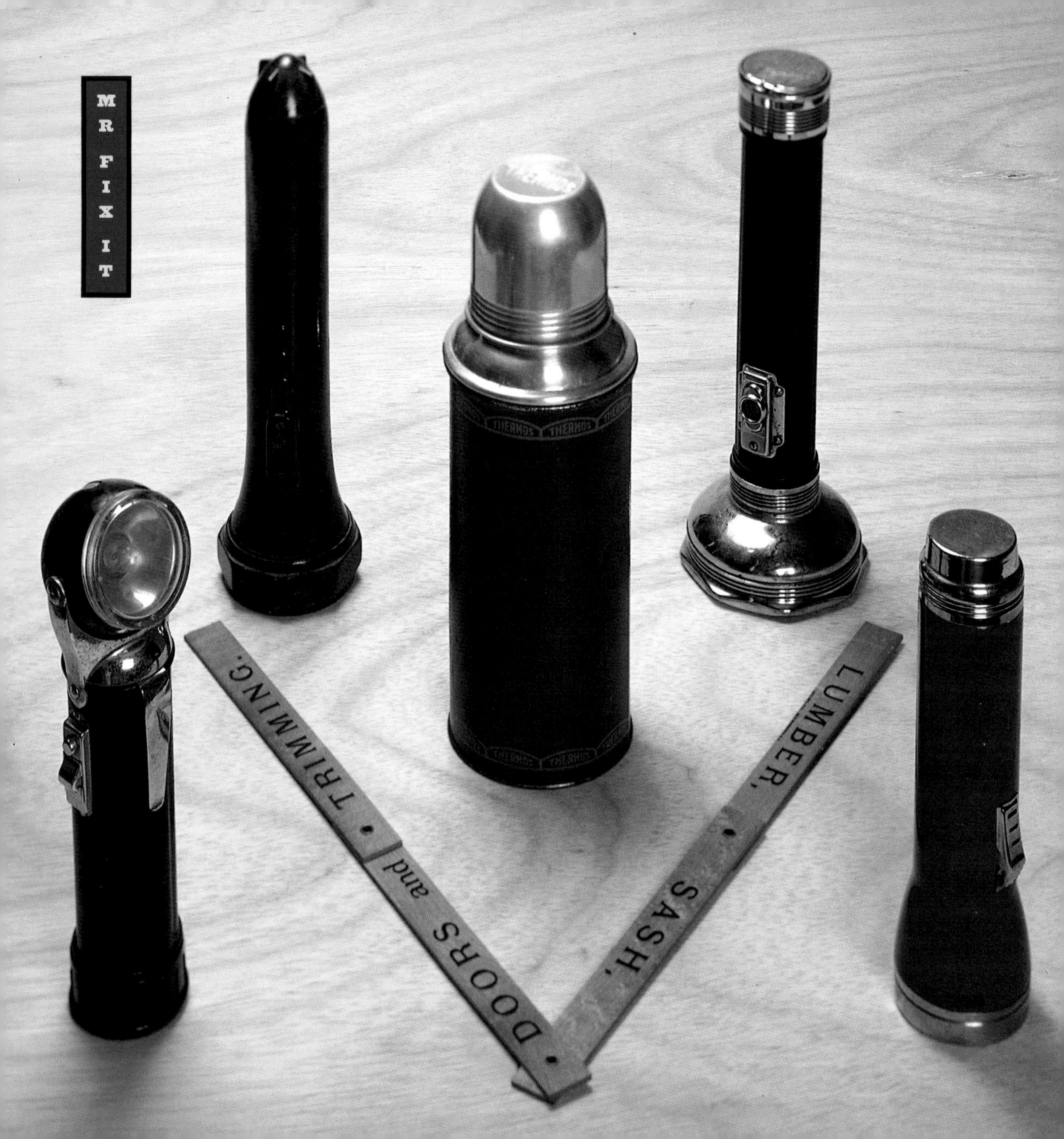

Basement workshops were prevalent in the thirties, but it wasn't until after WWII that they really became popular. We fixed the world and made *it* right, why not fix that broken runner on the rocker. Or put some paneling in the den. Lumber trucks were working overtime trying to supply two-by-fours and plywood to all the Mr. Fix Its puttering judiciously in basement shops across America; clamping, jigsawing, planing, gluing—making one hell of a mess and then daring anyone to deny they didn't come through. Ads to build everything from doghouses to cribs capitalized on this new-found obsession. Standing in the backyard, the kids beamed with pride as Dad secured the last bolt in the swingset. Meanwhile, Mom wasn't letting the kids do any swinging until Dad tested it first.

GIRLIE

T here were girls, and then there were Girlie Girls. Sleek and slender they peeked from under an unassuming tie or lounged luxuriantly on your cocktail glasses. Pick up a church key to open a beer, and you wrapped your hand around a languorous dame, her legs stretched out, her arms clasped behind her head forming the slot to pry off the bottle cap.

The Girlie Girl was everywhere. Her wishes of winsome cheer enticed you on your birthday from the card your buddies sent. Or gussied up in Santa's robe, which usually covered Old Nick's substantial girth but barely makes it past her thigh, she blithely reaches up to hang a stocking over the fireplace and bid you a soft and warm and happy Yuletide. When she adorned the back of a deck, she made playing a game of cards require that much more concentration. And a drink packed extra punch when the glass which displayed her clothed (however scantily) on the outside, allowed a clear view of her lace and frills on the inside, once the intrusive beverage was consumed.

Like a figurehead on a ship, plaster Girlie sculptures adorned bookshelves and mantels, were mounted like *bas* reliefs on a bachelor's wall. Not quite like a hunter's big game trophies. More like Samplers, reminders of where one's attention should be when properly focused—eyes kept on the prize.

Men who didn't have a clue what day it was at home, knew precisely the year, month, date, the phases of the moon, even Flag Day, because an auburn-haired beauty was resplendent on their calendar at the office. And other fellas who only called their mother once a year, sent their buddies postcards on a very regular basis—because on the card was a long-legged librarian in a petite skirt who loves to read, especially when the book is placed on the floor at her feet and she has to bend down to turn the pages.

Girlie Girls were always squeaky clean and always smiling. They seemed to never run out of reasons to joyfully bend over—to pick something up, put something down, to just stay happily limber. Their legs were long. Their skin fair. Their hair full of jubilant bounce. They seemed always dressed in their younger sister's clothes—shorts that didn't quite fit; blouses which, because of our Girlie Girl's more ample bosom, firmly tested the elasticity of the fabric. And though she blithely adorned many cocktail glasses and shakers, she herself never appeared with a drink. She lived a clean life, never got cold, and was always oh so, ever so happy to see you.

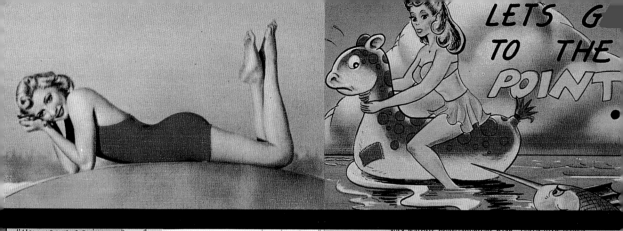

Here's a typical scene: woman holding back Girlie-smitten man. Even though she herself is a cutie, with freckles, big-eyes, cinch waist, and neatly-styled do, she's got no hips and her dress allows only a glimpse of gams. Her emanating love rays declare her fidelity and general acceptance of the eye-popping Wow-Factor inherent in her man. That's a letter opener next to the happy couple. Something useful to have lying on the desk, even on Sunday, when there isn't any mail.

INDUSTRIAL
EQUIPMENT & SUPPLY
COMPANY
540 Minor St. - Phone 2-2191
READING, PENNA.

Dude and Nugget were among several men's magazines in the '40s and '50s that included a little skin between the articles. *Peep Show* was rumored to have been anonymously edited by Jacques Derrida as a forum to develop his Deconstructivist theories, but there is no hard evidence to back this up.

The inventor was all set to retire. He'd wrapped up all the attributes of the perfect woman and figured out a way to make her instantly appear. And this was *before* Tang! He would have sold millions, except the initial purchasers discovered one tiny flaw—once you created Instant Woman, there was no way to get rid of her.

The girl who was scared to death of a mouse now has a daughter who jumps at the chance to go out with a wolf

Lingerie:
Gay nighties

When it comes to spreading gossip, the female of the species is faster than the mail

...er own business

...he gal flirting with the... he found she was a teller... ...in the bank when the...

The Inalienable Life, Liberty and Happiness of Purs...

Bathing Suit:
Clothing cut
to See Level

GIRDLE: A device to keep an unfortunate situation from spreading

THE SOUND OF ONE HAND SPANKING

Truths. Axioms. Little Zen-like sayings. That's what a man needed to make some sense out of the mysterious workings of a woman's mind and other paradoxical aspects of the universe. And what better place to put them than on a cocktail napkin, the one literary source a man was most apt to pay attention to. Taken in their entirety, the cocktail napkin *oeuvre* codified into pithy maxims a set of guidelines to make the world a less ambiguous place—justifying the fact that most of the time men walked around completely baffled. And after tossing down a few drinks and trying out (unsuccessfully) a few of their "best lines," the gents at the bar were more than willing to believe what they read printed on a flimsy piece of tissue paper marked with rings of condensation from the bottom of their glass.

hen you were a bachelor it didn't matter where you left your stuff. When you got married and had kids and everyone was poking into everything, you needed someplace safe, sacred, that was yours alone. Your top drawer. And within the household it quickly assumed the status of being a sanctuary—Dad's top dresser drawer. And no wayward hands, neither spouse nor progeny, ventured into that holy domain.

Not all of it was worth guarding. Stuff like sock garters lived toward the back. As did a few pairs of underwear you'd grown out of. Widowed socks took up a lot of space. Out-of-style braces. Hardly exotic. Hardly worth hiding. But there was also treasure.

Cufflinks. Tie clips. A matching set or two, in the faux-felt box that shut fast with a fierce, resounding snap meant to intimidate any curious little fingers from investigating. Other little jewelry boxes housed the everyday links and clips, along with a stray stud (unused for a decade), some shark's teeth, a buffalo nickel, and, perhaps, some souvenirs picked up at a National Monument or two.

Not keen on knick-knacks, what few you have also reside in The Drawer. Scraps of seemingly meaningless paper. A matchbook with a phone number inside. "Call anytime for a super deal on a set of whitewalls." Ticket stubs—from prize fights, ball games, a Daily Double where your horse Placed in the Second race, goddamit.

You've got your condoms in there, too. Even though the kids could find them, if they pulled the drawer out as far as it would go and Red Sea-ed the socks. But this is where condoms are supposed to go, and you can't break with tradition. And some day your oldest kid will find them, and then one thing will lead to another, and suddenly it is time for the Big Talk.

It's like a scrapbook, this drawer. Full of remembrances of things past. Bow ties that seemed like a good idea at the time, now still in their packages. A pipe you tried on a disastrous first date (Oh God, that *pipe!*). A broken watch. Aviator goggles you donned on surveillance missions over Sicily. Buttons from the overcoat you wore all through college, flask tucked into the inside pocket. Now threadbare, donated to Goodwill.

There's lots of stuff you should throw away. But the memories are too vivid. A strip of photo booth snapshots of you and a best friend, in the totem pole pose, his name is . . . Jesus, look how thin you are, and how much hair you had. His phone number's on the back—the exchange written out "Bigelow 4 . . ." How long has it been?

And if you were lucky enough to have any stuff handed down to you from your dad, this is likely where you keep it. His wallet perhaps, somehow still bearing his smell. Maybe one of his handkerchiefs, his initials in the corner. There are a few of your own in there, too. Why can't you remember to carry one?

And if you were really lucky, truly blessed, you may have your father's or your grandfather's pocket watch. It hasn't worked in decades, but you know some day you really will give its works a cleaning and polish the outside, so even if you don't carry it, it will make that much more of an impression when it's time to pass it on to your kid.

NO MATTER HOW YOU

TWIST

OR

TURN

Don't be a
"CURLY
COLLAR"

Neck Zone *Stays* Put

*NECK ZONE means smooth shoulders, perfect drape,

"Hi Honey."
"Hi Dear."
"Look, I'm running a little late here at the office."
"Again?"
"Now Honey, don't . . . "
"How late will you be?"
"Well, let me see, by my watch it's 6:43 and Miss Curtis and I have just a *ton* of work we have to . . . Honey? Honey!??"

"Vivian!! Howaya! It's Big Al, your favorite salesman, ready to show you the Spring line. And boy! Have I got some winners that will . . . "
"Hello, Al. I thought you weren't coming."
"But it's 3:00! On the button! My usual time! The same every season! Big Al's 3:00 appointment!"
"It's 4:20, Al."
"BUT It can't be. My watch . . . My watch says . . . My watch says . . . 3:00."

"Hey Charlie."
"Yeah?"
"You see the boss checking his watch when you came in this morning?"
"What about it?"
"I'd watch it if I were you. It's the second day this week you've been late."
"Ahh, tell the old coot he can blow it out his ear."

"You really should go."
"Mmmmm."
"It's late."
"Mmmm. Yes. I know."
"What time is it?"
"I can't move my arm."
"What if I . . . "
"A little more. There, now I can . . . "
"Wait. Mmmnnn. It can't be *that* late. It just can't."

SPARE TIME? DON'T KNOW WHAT TO DO? CHECK YOUR TIE CLIP.

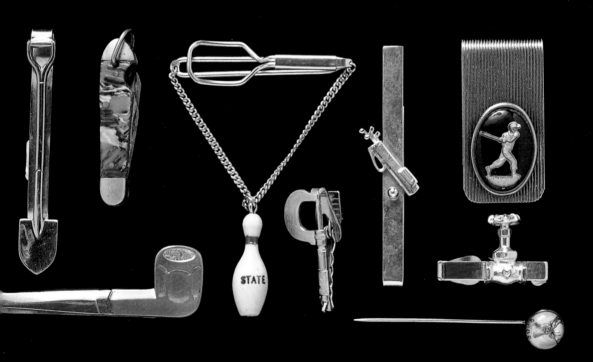

Because most of the buyers were women, if you were a travelling salesman
it mattered how you were groomed. Your first impression
when you arrived for your appointment was just as important as any of
the samples you took out to show her. Because only if everything
was perfectly in place—

1 **HAIR SLEEKED BACK,**

2 **CHEEK AND CHIN SMOOTHLY SHAVEN,**

3 **HAIR FINE-TUNED WITH THE BRUSH,**

4 **ODORS DEODORIZED INTO SUBMISSION,**

5 **TEETH BRUSHED AND YOUR BREATH SWEET—**

only *then* would you make an *impression*, and have a chance to
land yourself a big order. And since the hotel didn't supply you with anything
more than a sink, you had to bring your own kit with you.
It might also include a nail file and clipper, as she'll be watching your hands
as you write out the order. Razor, blades, and cologne travelled
separately in your suitcase.

And even if the buyers weren't women, when you're a salesman,
out there like Willy Loman, you've always got to look your best. Because
what else did you have? Just yourself. Just a smile and shoeshine.

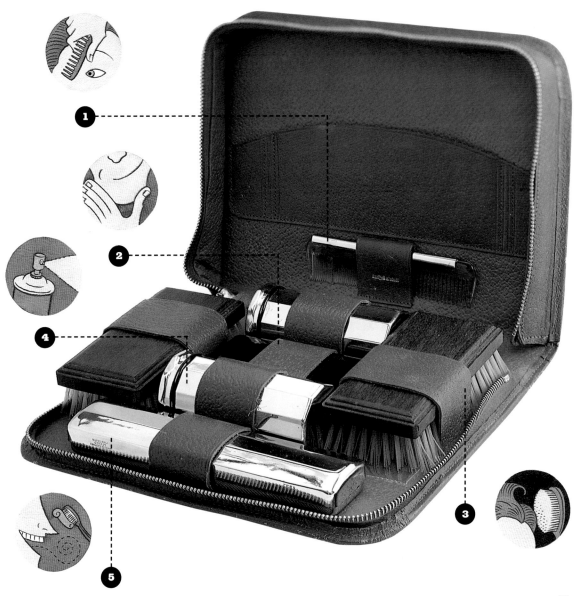

T here has always been more to smoking than simply cigarettes.

First of all, there were lighters. Pocket lighters sported scenes of favorite pastimes, from fly fishing to bowling. A pack a day meant twenty chances to remind yourself of what you'd rather be doing, except, of course, if you were actually doing it. Pocket lighters had a distinctive sound, the tinny "ching" of the top flipping open, like a hi-hat cymbal; the soft scrape of the wheel hitting the flint, like brushes on a snare. Together they were the instantly recognizable downbeat for your smoke.

Table lighters could be (and usually were) much larger objects, ingeniously devised in the shapes of yachts, pistols, airplanes, race horses, so your coffee table was a miniature emporium of Dreams Come True.

Anything with a dent became an ashtray. The brim of a cowboy hat, the center of a tire. Ashtrays were used more frequently than the refrigerator. They were often freebies, giveaways from salesmen, who felt certain they would become an essential object on a potential client's desk. Some ashtrays had side-tables built around them, kind of a "Smoking Center," with places for the cigarettes, a lighter or matches, and a handle on top so it could be set down next to any chair in the house.

Omnia meo cigaretum porto–"I carry all my butts with me." But how to keep them from being crushed? (This was pre-hard pack.) For elegant transport, one used a silver case. The cigarettes were removed from their pack and tucked into the inside of the covers. It was sort of like packing bullets into your gun which, you found out twenty years later, had been pointed at your lungs the whole time.

More prosaic plastic cases were also devised and functioned like an insect's ecto-skeleton, to protect the vital guts of the pack.

And then there were match books—so woven into the fabric of a man's life that the four words "Close Cover When Striking" were of greater everyday significance than "In God We Trust." A bowl of matchbooks was also a scrapbook, reminders of restaurants and hotels and bars you visited. You pick up one from the top of the pile, open it, and see a phone number that had been copied swiftly inside. Lighting the match also sparks a memory—a blissful tryst, perhaps, or a road not taken? You light your cigarette and shake out the flame. It's been too long to remember. You close the matchbook, take a deep drag, and toss it back in the bowl.

And along with the smoking hardware, there was also smoking style—a set of moves that needed to be deftly mastered in order to acquit oneself with élan. Moves like the One-Handed Soft-Pack Reveal, in which, through short upward jerks of the pack you coerced three cigarettes to emerge from the top of the pack. Or the Single-Handed Case Exposure and Presentation, where, in one motion, you retrieved your silver case from the inside pocket of your sport jacket, pressed the release button, guided the top open, and offered your paramour a cigarette. Or the Long-Distance Butt-flick, best performed in the wee small hours, after a light rain, the streetlight reflected in the dirty puddles, which was set up with a last deep drag before the butt was removed and flicked in an elegant arc into the street, and you turned up your collar, jammed your hands in your pockets, and started the slow walk home.

You must start early,
readying your lighter when
she's first fumbling through
her purse for her pack.
But don't reveal it too soon.
Stay suave. Wait until
she's removing the cigarette
from the pack. Keep
your arm loose and don't
crowd her. Ignite the
lighter away from her face,
and let her hand guide
it in. If she's swayed,
her eyes will linger on
yours. If not, just close
the lid, tip your hat,
and move on.

Think how our nervous, hurried way of living affects DIGESTION!

—for Digestion's Sake — Smoke Camels

"Hey Average Joe." "Yes Mr. Scientist?" "How's that pastrami sandwich sittin'?" "Well, to be honest, Sir, it's sittin' kinda heavy." "Here, try these." [Five cigarettes later.] "How's that stomach feelin' now?" "It's a miracle, Mr. Scientist, it feels . . . hack, hack, wheeze . . . a lot . . . aghh . . . better." "That's because you increased your alkalinity."

"Boy. Thanks, Mr. Scientist." "It's okay, Joe. I bet you're working hard, aren't you Joe, bringing home that bacon." "Sure am."

"You're nervous. Stressed." "That's me." "You owe it to your wife and kiddies to smoke as much as possible. To stimulate the ol' digestion. Keep that alkalinity level up." "I'll do my best, Mr. Scientist Sir." "I'm sure you will, Joe. I'm sure you will."

You're darn tootin my dad smokes *Marlboro* . . . he knows what's good for him!

Camels stimulate digestion in a pleasant, natural way... increase alkalinity!

The human digestion responds unfavorably to nervousness, hurry, and strain. It is definitely encouraged by smoking Camels. Scientific studies show clearly the manner in which Camels aid digestion. Using sensitive scientific apparatus, it is possible to measure accurately the increase in digestive fluids that follows the enjoyment of Camel's costlier tobaccos.

Make Camels your cigarette. Experience the sense of well-being they bring. For digestion's sake, enjoy Camels.

95

ACKNOWLEDGEMENTS

The authors are indebted to the following for their assistance in the writing of this book:
Archangel Antiques, New York; Harry Anderson, Philadelphia; Barry Berg, New York;
David Cohen, New York; Polly Dufresne, New York; the folks at Farfetched, New York;
Jennifer Greenblatt, New York; Helene and Paul Guarnaccia; Jessica Helfand;
Steve Heller; Kaleidoscope Books, Ann Arbor; Les Druyan, New York; Peter Masi;
Rage of the Age, Ann Arbor; Carol Sommers; Pam Sommers; Richard Sulzer;
Peter and Judy White of "Scout," New York.